The Business Model Blueprint:
A Step-by-Step Guide to Creating a Sustainable Business

Dan M. Savage

1

Table of contents

Introduction to Business Models

In the world of entrepreneurship, a business model is a fundamental concept that defines the way a company creates, delivers, and captures value. It outlines the strategy a company uses to generate revenue and profit, and to sustain its operations. A good business model is critical for any company seeking to build a successful and sustainable business.

In this chapter, we will explore the concept of business models, the various types of business models, and their role in building a successful company.

What is a Business Model?

A business model is a framework that outlines how a company creates and delivers value to its customers, and how it captures that value for itself in the form of revenue and profit. A business model comprises several components that are interdependent and work together to define the overall strategy of the company.

The Components of a Business Model

A business model typically consists of the following components:

Customer Segments: The target audience for the company's products or services. This could be a specific demographic, a particular industry, or a group of customers with similar needs.

Value Proposition: The unique value that the company's products or services offer to its customers. This could be a product's features, quality, price, or any other characteristic that sets it apart from the competition.

Channels: The methods through which the company delivers its products or services to its customers. This could be through online platforms, physical stores, or other means.

Customer Relationships: The ways in which the company interacts with its customers. This could be through personal interactions, online forums, or other channels.

Revenue Streams: The ways in which the company generates revenue, such as through product sales, subscriptions, or advertising.

Key Activities: The critical activities required to deliver the company's products or services to its customers.

Key Resources: The resources required to operate the company, such as personnel, equipment, or intellectual property.

Key Partnerships: The strategic partnerships that the company has established to deliver its products or services. This could include suppliers, distributors, or other companies.

Cost Structure: The costs associated with operating the company, including fixed costs and variable costs.

Types of Business Models

There are several types of business models, each with its own unique characteristics and strategies. Some of the most common business models include:

B2C (Business-to-Consumer): A business model that focuses on selling products or services directly to individual consumers.

B2B (Business-to-Business): A business model that focuses on selling products or services to other businesses.

Marketplace: A business model that brings together buyers and sellers in a common platform, and takes a commission on each transaction.

Subscription: A business model that offers products or services to customers on a recurring basis, typically for a monthly or annual fee.

Freemium: A business model that offers a basic product or service for free, but charges for premium features.

Platform: A business model that creates a platform for other companies to build their businesses on.

The Role of Business Models in Building a Successful Company

A good business model is critical for building a successful company. It provides a roadmap for the company's strategy, and helps ensure that the company is creating and delivering value to its customers in the most effective way possible. A good business model also helps the company to identify potential areas of growth and expansion, and to manage costs and resources effectively.

Conclusion

In conclusion, a business model is a critical component of building a successful company. It outlines the strategy that a company uses to create, deliver, and capture value, and provides a framework for managing costs, resources, and growth. By understanding the different types of business models and their components, entrepreneurs can create a business model.

Chapter 1

Customer Segments

One of the key elements of any successful business is the ability to understand and serve the needs of its customers. Customer segments are groups of customers that share similar needs, characteristics, or behaviors. By identifying and targeting specific customer segments, businesses can tailor their products, services, and marketing efforts to meet the unique needs of each segment, leading to increased customer satisfaction and loyalty.

Identifying Customer Segments

The first step in identifying customer segments is to conduct market research to gain an understanding of the different groups of customers that exist in the marketplace. This can be done through a variety of methods, including surveys, focus groups, and online research.

Once you have collected this information, it is important to analyze it to identify patterns and group customers into segments based on common needs, behaviors, or other characteristics. Some common ways to segment customers include demographic factors such as age, gender, and income, as well as psychographic factors such as values, interests, and lifestyle.

Creating Customer Profiles

Once you have identified your customer segments, the next step is to create a customer profile for each segment. A customer profile is a detailed description of the characteristics and needs of a specific customer segment. This profile should include information such as their age, gender, income, education, values, interests, and buying behaviors.

To create a customer profile, businesses can use a variety of techniques, such as customer surveys, interviews, and online research. The goal is to create a detailed picture of the customer segment, including their needs, preferences, and pain points. This information can then be used to tailor marketing messages and product offerings to meet the unique needs of each segment.

Tailoring Marketing Messages

One of the key benefits of creating customer segments and profiles is the ability to tailor marketing messages to each segment. By understanding the unique needs and preferences of each segment, businesses can create targeted marketing campaigns that resonate with customers and drive engagement.

For example, if a business is targeting a customer segment that is price-sensitive, they may want to highlight the value and affordability of their products in their marketing messages. On the other hand, if they are targeting a segment that is focused on sustainability, they may want to highlight the eco-friendliness of their products and their commitment to reducing their environmental impact.

Tailoring Product Offerings

In addition to tailoring marketing messages, customer segments can also be used to tailor product offerings. By understanding the unique needs and preferences of each segment, businesses can develop products and services that meet those needs and provide a better customer experience.

For example, if a business is targeting a customer segment that is focused on convenience, they may want to offer a mobile app that allows customers to easily order products and track their shipments.

On the other hand, if they are targeting a segment that values luxury, they may want to develop high-end products with premium materials and exclusive designs.

Conclusion

Customer segments are a powerful tool for businesses looking to better understand and serve their customers. By identifying and targeting specific customer segments, businesses can tailor their marketing messages and product offerings to meet the unique needs of each segment, leading to increased customer satisfaction and loyalty. By taking the time to create detailed customer profiles and understanding the unique characteristics of each segment, businesses can stay ahead of the competition and build long-lasting relationships with their customers.

Chapter 2

Value Proposition

The value proposition is the essence of a company's business model. It describes the unique value that a business offers to its customers, and why they should choose it over its competitors. A well-crafted value proposition can help a company stand out in a crowded market, attract and retain customers, and ultimately drive revenue growth.

Creating a compelling value proposition requires a deep understanding of your customers' needs and preferences, as well as an understanding of the competitive landscape. In this chapter, we will explore the key elements of a value proposition, and provide a step-by-step guide for creating a unique and compelling value proposition that resonates with your target customers.

What is a Value Proposition?

A value proposition is a clear statement that describes the unique value that a company offers to its customers. It explains how the company's products or services solve a particular problem or meet a specific need, and why they are better than the competition.

A good value proposition should be:

Clear: The value proposition should be concise and easy to understand. It should clearly articulate the benefits that the company offers to its customers.

Unique: The value proposition should differentiate the company from its competitors. It should clearly explain why the company's products or services are better than those of its competitors.

Compelling: The value proposition should be convincing and appealing to the target customers. It should speak to their needs and desires.

Key Elements of a Value Proposition

There are four key elements of a value proposition: customer, problem, solution, and differentiation. Let's explore each of these elements in more detail.

Customer: Who are the target customers? What are their needs, preferences, and pain points?

Problem: What specific problem or need does the customer have that the company can solve?

Solution: How does the company's product or service solve the customer's problem or meet their need?

Differentiation: What makes the company's solution unique and better than the competition?

Step-by-Step Guide to Creating a Compelling Value Proposition

Identify your target customers: To create a compelling value proposition, you need to know who your target customers are. Who are they? What are their needs and preferences? What are their pain points?

Identify the problem: Once you have identified your target customers, you need to identify the specific problem or need that your product or service solves. What pain point does your product or service address? How does it make your customer's life easier or better?

Develop the solution: Once you have identified the problem, you need to develop a solution that solves it. How does your product or service address the pain point? What features or benefits does it offer that make it a better solution than the competition?

Differentiate from the competition: To create a compelling value proposition, you need to differentiate your solution from the competition. What makes your product or service unique? What benefits does it offer that the competition does not? Why should customers choose your solution over the competition?

Test and refine: Once you have developed your value proposition, it's important to test it with your target customers. Get feedback and refine your value proposition until it resonates with your target customers.

Examples of Compelling Value Propositions

Here are a few examples of compelling value propositions:

Apple: "Think Different" - Apple's value proposition is built around innovation and creativity. The company's products are designed to inspire and enable customers to create, learn, and express themselves in new ways.

Netflix: "Watch TV shows and movies anytime, anywhere, personalized for you" - Netflix's value proposition is built around convenience and personalization. The company's streaming service allows customers to watch their favorite TV shows and movies anytime, anywhere.

Chapter 3

Channels

Channels are the various ways in which a business can reach and communicate with its customers. A channel can be defined as any means of communication that a company uses to deliver its value proposition to its customers. In today's digital age, businesses have more channels than ever to reach their customers, both online and offline.

Online Channels

The internet has completely revolutionized the way businesses can communicate with their customers. The following are some of the most common online channels:

Website: A website is a key online channel for businesses. A website is the first place that customers will look to learn more about a company, its products and services, and its value proposition. Businesses need to ensure that their website is easy to navigate, mobile-friendly, and provides a seamless user experience.

Social Media: Social media platforms like Facebook, Twitter, Instagram, and LinkedIn provide businesses with a powerful way to reach and engage with their customers. Social media can be used to build brand awareness, drive traffic to a website, and engage customers in a conversation.

Email: Email is still one of the most effective channels for businesses to communicate with their customers. Email marketing campaigns can be used to promote products and services, offer discounts, and keep customers informed about new developments and changes in the business.

Blogging: A blog is a great way to create content that can help educate customers about a company's products and services. Blogs can also be used to build thought leadership and establish a business as an authority in its industry.

Offline Channels

While online channels are powerful, offline channels are still important for many businesses. The following are some of the most common offline channels:

In-person: In-person channels include face-to-face interactions, such as meetings, events, and conferences. These channels can be used to build relationships with customers and partners, and to showcase products and services.

Print: Print channels include advertising in newspapers and magazines, as well as direct mail campaigns. While print advertising is declining in popularity, it can still be effective for businesses that want to target a specific audience.

Broadcasting: Broadcasting channels include television and radio advertising. While these channels can be expensive, they can be effective for businesses that want to reach a large audience.

Choosing the Right Channels

Choosing the right channels for a business depends on a variety of factors, including the business's target audience, its budget, and its goals. The following are some tips for choosing the right channels:

Know Your Audience: Businesses need to understand their target audience and how they like to be communicated with. This will help businesses to choose the right channels to reach and engage their customers.

Test and Measure: Businesses need to test different channels to see what works and what doesn't. They should also measure the success of each channel to determine which channels are most effective.

Be Strategic: Businesses should choose channels that align with their overall strategy and goals. They should also consider the strengths and weaknesses of each channel, and how they can be used to achieve the business's objectives.

Conclusion

Channels are a critical component of a business's marketing strategy. Choosing the right channels can help businesses to reach and engage their customers, both online and offline. By understanding their audience, testing and measuring different channels, and being strategic, businesses can create a powerful and effective channel strategy that supports their overall business goals.

Chapter 4

Customer Relationships

In the world of business, it is widely acknowledged that building strong customer relationships is key to achieving success. Not only do satisfied customers drive repeat business, but they also serve as brand ambassadors, spreading the word about a company's products and services to their network. In this chapter, we will explore the different types of customer relationships and how businesses can create and maintain them.

Understanding Customer Relationships
Customer relationships are built on a foundation of trust, transparency, and communication. It is the relationship between the business and its customers that determines how successful the business will

be. There are four types of customer relationships that businesses can develop:

Basic transactional relationships: In this type of relationship, customers simply purchase a product or service from a business without any ongoing communication or engagement. This is the most basic type of customer relationship and is not particularly effective in building long-term customer loyalty.

Reactive relationships: In this type of relationship, businesses respond to customers only when there is a problem or issue. This type of relationship is reactive in nature and does not provide an opportunity for businesses to proactively engage with customers.

Proactive relationships: This type of relationship is more engaging, as businesses proactively reach out to customers with relevant information, advice, and support.

This type of relationship is effective in building customer loyalty and long-term relationships.

Partnership relationships: This is the most advanced type of customer relationship, in which businesses work closely with their customers to understand their needs, provide customized solutions, and create value for both parties.

Creating Strong Customer Relationships
To create strong customer relationships, businesses need to invest time and resources in understanding their customers, their needs, and their preferences. Here are some ways businesses can do this:

Listen to customer feedback: Customers provide valuable feedback that can help businesses improve their products, services, and customer experience. Businesses should actively solicit feedback and use it to inform their business decisions.

Personalize the customer experience: Customers appreciate personalized experiences that make them feel valued and appreciated. Businesses can use data and insights to personalize their interactions with customers and provide tailored solutions that meet their unique needs.

Build trust and credibility: Trust is the foundation of any strong relationship, and businesses need to be transparent, honest, and reliable to build trust with their customers. Credibility can be built through consistent performance, delivering on promises, and providing a quality customer experience.

Maintaining Strong Customer Relationships
Once businesses have established strong customer relationships, it is important to maintain them. Here are some ways businesses can do this:

Continue to engage with customers: Businesses should continue to engage with customers through regular communication, updates, and relevant content. This can help to keep the relationship active and maintain customer loyalty.

Provide ongoing support: Businesses should be proactive in providing ongoing support to their customers, helping them to solve problems, and addressing any issues that arise.

Reward customer loyalty: Businesses should recognize and reward customer loyalty, offering incentives, rewards, and exclusive offers to long-term customers.

Conclusion
Building strong customer relationships is critical to the success of any business. By understanding the different types of customer relationships, businesses can create effective strategies to engage with

their customers, build trust and credibility, and provide ongoing support. Maintaining strong customer relationships requires ongoing effort and investment, but the benefits of doing so are significant, including increased customer loyalty, repeat business, and positive word of mouth.

Chapter 5

Revenue Streams

One of the most important aspects of building a successful business is identifying and developing a reliable revenue stream. Revenue streams refer to the ways in which businesses generate income. In this chapter, we will explore different revenue streams and how they can be used to drive growth and profitability.

Types of Revenue Streams

There are several types of revenue streams that businesses can use to generate income. Some of the most common types of revenue streams include:

Product Sales: This is the most traditional way of generating revenue, where a business sells a physical or digital product to its customers. This can include anything from consumer goods to software products.

Subscription Fees: This revenue stream involves charging customers a recurring fee for access to a service or product. This can include anything from magazine subscriptions to software-as-a-service (SaaS) products.

Advertising: This revenue stream involves businesses generating income by displaying ads on their platform or website. This can include anything from banner ads to native advertising.

Affiliate Marketing: This revenue stream involves businesses earning a commission for promoting or recommending a product or service to their audience. This can include anything from recommending products on social media to creating affiliate marketing partnerships with other businesses.

Licensing and Franchising: This revenue stream involves businesses generating income by licensing their intellectual property, technology, or products to other businesses. This can include anything from franchising a restaurant to licensing a software product.

Choosing the Right Revenue Stream

Choosing the right revenue stream is critical to the success of any business. The right revenue stream should align with the business's goals and be sustainable over the long term. Here are some factors to consider when choosing a revenue stream:

Value Proposition: The revenue stream should align with the business's value proposition and core offering. For example, a software company that sells enterprise software may choose to generate revenue through subscription fees, while a consumer goods company may choose to generate revenue through product sales.

Customer Segment: The revenue stream should be tailored to the business's target customer segment. For example, a business targeting enterprise customers may choose to generate revenue through subscription fees, while a business targeting consumers may choose to generate revenue through product sales or advertising.

Competition: The revenue stream should be differentiated from the competition. For example, a business in a crowded market may choose to generate revenue through affiliate marketing or licensing, rather than product sales or subscription fees.

Scalability: The revenue stream should be scalable and able to support the growth of the business. For example, a business that relies on physical product sales may face challenges scaling their revenue stream beyond a certain point, while a business that relies on subscription fees may be able to scale more easily.

Cost Structure: The revenue stream should be aligned with the business's cost structure. For example, a business with high fixed costs may choose to generate revenue through subscription fees, while a business with low fixed costs may choose to generate revenue through product sales or advertising.

Conclusion

In conclusion, choosing the right revenue stream is critical to the success of any business. By considering factors such as value proposition, customer segment, competition, scalability, and cost structure, businesses can identify the revenue stream that aligns with their goals and drives long-term growth and profitability. By exploring different revenue streams and understanding their benefits and drawbacks, businesses can make informed decisions about how to generate revenue and achieve success.

Chapter 6

Key Activities

When it comes to building a successful business, delivering on your value proposition is critical. The value proposition represents the unique value that your company provides to your customers and it is the foundation upon which your entire business model is built. However, to deliver on this value proposition, there are several key activities that a business must undertake. In this chapter, we will explore these key activities and discuss how they can be leveraged to create and deliver value to your customers.

Defining Key Activities

Key activities are the critical operations and processes that a business must undertake to create and deliver its value proposition.

They are the specific activities that a company performs to achieve its business objectives and deliver value to its customers. Key activities can vary depending on the nature of the business and the specific value proposition that the company is offering.

For example, if your business is focused on manufacturing and selling products, your key activities might include product design, sourcing materials, manufacturing, and distribution. If your business is focused on providing services, your key activities might include marketing, customer acquisition, service delivery, and customer support.

Identifying Key Activities

To identify your business's key activities, start by defining your value proposition. This will help you understand the specific activities that are necessary to create and deliver that value. Once you have a clear understanding of your value proposition, you can start to identify the key activities that are critical to achieving it.

It's important to note that not all activities are key activities. Some activities may be necessary for the operation of your business, but they may not be critical to delivering your value proposition. By identifying your key activities, you can focus your resources and efforts on the activities that will have the greatest impact on your business.

Managing Key Activities

Managing key activities involves developing processes and systems to ensure that these activities are performed efficiently and effectively. This may involve streamlining processes, automating tasks, or outsourcing certain activities to third-party providers.

In addition, it's important to continuously evaluate your key activities to ensure that they are still relevant and effective. As your business grows and evolves, your key activities may change, and you may need to adjust your processes and systems accordingly.

Examples of Key Activities

Here are some examples of key activities that a business might undertake:

Product Development: If your business is focused on developing new products, your key activities might include market research, product design, and prototyping.

Marketing and Sales: If your business is focused on selling products or services, your key activities might include market research, lead generation, sales, and customer support.

Service Delivery: If your business is focused on providing services, your key activities might include customer acquisition, service delivery, and customer support.

Manufacturing: If your business is focused on manufacturing products, your key activities might include sourcing materials, manufacturing, and distribution.

Conclusion

In conclusion, key activities are critical to delivering on your value proposition and achieving your business objectives. By identifying and managing your key activities, you can ensure that your business is focused on the activities that will have the greatest impact on your success. It's important to continuously evaluate and adjust your key activities to ensure that they remain relevant and effective as your business evolves.

Chapter 7

Key Resources

In the world of business, resources are the essential building blocks of success. Without the right resources, a business cannot create and deliver its value proposition, nor can it sustain its operations in the long term. Key resources are the critical elements that enable a business to operate and grow, and they can take many forms, such as employees, technology, or capital.

In this chapter, we will explore the importance of key resources and how businesses can identify, acquire, and manage them to achieve their goals.

The Role of Key Resources in Creating Value

At its core, a business exists to create and deliver value to its customers. Key resources are the essential elements that enable a business to do this. For example, a restaurant needs skilled chefs, fresh ingredients, and modern kitchen equipment to create high-quality meals. A software company needs talented programmers, up-to-date hardware, and innovative software tools to create cutting-edge software products.

Identifying Key Resources

To identify the key resources that a business needs, it is essential to understand the value proposition and the customer segments that the business is targeting. For example, a business that is targeting high-end customers will need to invest in premium resources, such as luxurious facilities or top-notch personnel, to create a premium experience. In contrast, a business that is targeting a more budget-conscious customer segment may focus on more affordable resources, such as low-cost facilities or personnel.

Acquiring Key Resources

Acquiring key resources can be a significant challenge for a business, particularly for startups or small businesses. There are several ways to acquire key resources, including hiring employees, acquiring technology or equipment, or raising capital.

Hiring Employees

Hiring the right employees is critical to the success of any business. Hiring the wrong employees can be costly in terms of time, money, and resources, as well as detrimental to a business's culture and morale. It is essential to identify the specific skills, experience, and personality traits that are needed for each position and to conduct a thorough screening and selection process.

Acquiring Technology or Equipment

Technology and equipment are critical resources for many businesses, particularly those in the manufacturing or technology industries. These resources can be expensive, so it is important to conduct a cost-benefit analysis and determine the best approach to acquire them. For example, a business may choose to lease equipment or purchase used equipment rather than investing in new equipment to reduce costs.

Raising Capital

Capital is another critical resource for many businesses. Raising capital can take many forms, such as taking out loans, seeking investment from venture capitalists or angel investors, or crowdfunding. Each method has its pros and cons, and it is important to select the most appropriate approach for each business's specific needs.

Managing Key Resources

Once a business has acquired its key resources, it is essential to manage them effectively. Effective resource management involves maintaining and optimizing resources to ensure that they continue to support the business's value proposition and goals.

Some key considerations for managing resources include:

Allocating resources effectively: Resources should be allocated based on the business's priorities and objectives.
Monitoring resource utilization: Businesses should track resource utilization to ensure that they are being used efficiently and effectively.
Planning for growth: Businesses should plan for future growth and identify the resources that will be needed to support that growth.

Developing contingency plans: Businesses should develop contingency plans to address any resource shortages or emergencies that may arise.

Conclusion

Key resources are the foundation of a successful business. Businesses must identify, acquire, and manage these resources effectively to create and deliver their value proposition, sustain their operations, and achieve their goals. By understanding the role of key resources and following best practices for identifying, acquiring, and managing them, businesses can build a solid foundation for long-term success.

Chapter 8

Key Partnerships

As a business owner, it's important to understand that you don't have to do everything alone. In fact, forming partnerships can be an effective way to leverage resources and expertise that you may not have in-house. These partnerships can help your business create and deliver its value proposition more effectively, allowing you to focus on your core competencies and differentiate yourself from the competition.

In this chapter, we will explore the different types of partnerships that a business can form, and how they can help you create and deliver value to your customers.

Types of Partnerships

There are several types of partnerships that a business can form. Here are a few of the most common types:

Supplier Partnerships: These partnerships involve working closely with suppliers to ensure that you have a reliable supply of the goods and services that you need to create your products or services.

Strategic Partnerships: These partnerships are formed with other businesses that have complementary products or services, or similar target markets. The goal is to leverage each other's strengths to create a mutually beneficial relationship.

Marketing Partnerships: These partnerships involve working with other businesses to promote your products or services. This could include co-branding, co-marketing, or joint advertising campaigns.

Joint Ventures: A joint venture is a formal agreement between two or more businesses to work together on a specific project or initiative. This could include joint product development, joint marketing campaigns, or shared research and development.

Distribution Partnerships: These partnerships involve working with other businesses to distribute your products or services. This could include partnerships with retailers, wholesalers, or distributors.

Technology Partnerships: These partnerships involve working with other businesses to develop new technologies or to integrate existing technologies into your products or services.

Why Form Partnerships?

There are several reasons why a business might choose to form partnerships. Some of the most common reasons include:

Access to expertise: Partnering with another business can give you access to specialized expertise that you may not have in-house.

Access to resources: Partnerships can provide you with access to resources that you may not have, such as manufacturing facilities, distribution networks, or research and development capabilities.

Risk sharing: By forming partnerships, you can share the risks and costs associated with new initiatives or projects.

New market opportunities: Partnering with another business can help you expand your market reach and access new customer segments.

Cost savings: Partnerships can help you reduce costs by sharing resources and expertise.

Choosing the Right Partnerships

When choosing partners, it's important to consider several factors, including:

Strategic fit: Look for partners that have complementary products or services, or a similar target market. This will help you leverage each other's strengths and create a mutually beneficial relationship.

Trust: Choose partners that you trust and that share your values. This will help ensure a successful partnership and avoid any potential conflicts.

Resources: Consider the resources that your partner can bring to the table, such as manufacturing facilities, distribution networks, or research and development capabilities.

Expertise: Look for partners that have specialized expertise that you may not have in-house. This will help you access new knowledge and skills.

Goals: Ensure that your partner's goals align with your own. This will help ensure that you are both working towards the same objectives.

Conclusion

Forming partnerships can be a powerful way to help your business create and deliver its value proposition. By leveraging the expertise, resources, and knowledge of other businesses, you can gain a competitive advantage and differentiate yourself from the competition. When choosing partners, it's important to consider factors such as strategic fit, trust, resources, expertise, and goals, to ensure a successful partnership that benefits both parties.

Chapter 9

Cost Structure

Cost structure is a critical aspect of any business, and it refers to the types and amounts of expenses that are incurred in creating and delivering a company's value proposition. Understanding the cost structure of a business is essential for ensuring that it is profitable and sustainable over the long term. In this chapter, we will explore the different costs that are associated with creating and delivering a business's value proposition and discuss strategies for managing those costs effectively.

Types of Costs
There are several different types of costs that a business incurs in creating and delivering its value proposition. These can include:

Fixed costs: These are expenses that do not vary with the level of production or sales. Examples of fixed costs include rent, salaries, insurance, and equipment.

Variable costs: These are expenses that vary with the level of production or sales. Examples of variable costs include raw materials, labor, and shipping costs.

Semi-variable costs: These are expenses that have both fixed and variable components. Examples of semi-variable costs include utilities and maintenance costs.

Direct costs: These are expenses that are directly associated with the production of a product or service. Examples of direct costs include raw materials, labor, and shipping costs.

Indirect costs: These are expenses that are not directly associated with the production of a product or service but are necessary for the business to operate. Examples of indirect costs include rent, utilities, and marketing expenses.

Managing Costs

Managing costs effectively is critical for the success of any business. Here are some strategies that businesses can use to manage their costs:

Analyze costs: Businesses should regularly analyze their costs to identify areas where they can reduce expenses or improve efficiency. This can be done by conducting a cost-benefit analysis of each activity or process and identifying opportunities for improvement.

Negotiate with suppliers: Businesses should negotiate with suppliers to get the best possible price for raw materials and other supplies. This can involve bulk purchasing or establishing long-term relationships with suppliers.

Streamline processes: Businesses should identify and eliminate any unnecessary steps or processes that increase costs. This can involve automating certain processes or reorganizing workflows to improve efficiency.

Monitor inventory: Businesses should monitor their inventory levels to avoid overstocking or understocking. Overstocking can lead to higher storage and maintenance costs, while understocking can result in lost sales and lower customer satisfaction.

Outsource non-core activities: Businesses can reduce costs by outsourcing non-core activities, such as accounting, IT support, or customer service, to specialized service providers.

Embrace technology: Technology can help businesses reduce costs by automating processes, improving efficiency, and reducing the need for manual labor. Businesses should explore the use of technology in areas such as production, inventory management, and customer service.

Conclusion
In conclusion, cost structure is a critical aspect of any business, and managing costs effectively is essential for ensuring long-term profitability and sustainability. By analyzing costs, negotiating with suppliers, streamlining processes, monitoring inventory, outsourcing non-core activities, and embracing technology, businesses can reduce their expenses and improve their bottom line. Understanding and managing cost structure is an ongoing process, and businesses should regularly review and adjust their strategies to ensure that they remain competitive and profitable.

Chapter 10

Scaling Your Business

Once a business has established a successful business model, it is important to think about how to scale it. Scaling a business means growing it beyond its current state, expanding its operations, and increasing its revenue. Scaling requires careful planning and the implementation of strategies that align with the company's goals and vision.

In this chapter, we will explore different strategies for scaling a business, including partnerships, acquisitions, and new markets. We will discuss the benefits and challenges of each approach and provide guidance on how to choose the best strategy for your business.

Partnerships

One of the most common strategies for scaling a business is through partnerships. A partnership is a relationship between two or more businesses that work together to achieve a common goal. Partnerships can take many forms, from joint ventures to strategic alliances. The key to a successful partnership is finding a partner whose strengths complement your own.

Partnering with another business can help you reach new customers, expand your product or service offerings, and reduce costs. It can also give you access to new markets and resources, such as technology or expertise. However, partnerships can also be risky, and it is important to do your due diligence and establish clear terms and expectations upfront.

Acquisitions

Acquisitions are another strategy for scaling a business. An acquisition is when one company buys another. Acquisitions can help you quickly gain access to new markets, customers, and technology. They can also eliminate competition and increase your market share.

Acquisitions can be a risky and expensive strategy, but if done correctly, they can provide significant benefits. Before pursuing an acquisition, it is important to thoroughly research the target company and ensure that the acquisition aligns with your long-term goals.

New Markets

Expanding into new markets is another way to scale your business. This can include entering new geographic markets, targeting new customer segments, or developing new products or services. Expanding into new markets can help you diversify your revenue streams and reduce your dependence on any one market.

Expanding into new markets can also be challenging. It requires a thorough understanding of the market and its dynamics, as well as the ability to adapt your business model to meet the needs of a new customer base.

Choosing the Right Strategy

Choosing the right scaling strategy for your business depends on a variety of factors, including your goals, resources, and capabilities. Before deciding on a strategy, it is important to conduct a thorough analysis of your business and the market, identify potential risks and challenges, and develop a plan that aligns with your long-term vision.

Some businesses may find that a combination of strategies, such as partnerships and acquisitions, is the most effective way to scale their business. Others may focus on organic growth, using their existing resources and capabilities to expand into new markets.

Conclusion

Scaling your business is a critical step in achieving long-term success. Whether you choose to partner with other businesses, pursue acquisitions, or expand into new markets, it is important to carefully consider your options and choose a strategy that aligns with your goals and vision. By following these guidelines, you can develop a scalable and sustainable business model that will help you achieve your business objectives.

Chapter 11

Innovation

Innovation is the lifeblood of any successful company in today's rapidly changing business environment. Organizations that prioritize innovation are better able to adapt to shifting customer needs, anticipate new market trends, and stay ahead of their competitors. In this chapter, we'll explore the importance of innovation and different approaches that companies can take to promote it, including design thinking and lean startup.

The Importance of Innovation
Innovation is critical for the long-term success of any company. It allows organizations to create new products, services, and business models that meet the changing needs of customers and address emerging market trends. Companies that

fail to innovate risk becoming irrelevant as their competitors disrupt the market with new and better solutions.

Innovation can take many forms, from incremental improvements to existing products to entirely new business models. It requires a willingness to take risks, experiment, and embrace failure as a learning opportunity. In today's fast-paced business environment, companies must be nimble and adaptable to stay relevant, and innovation is a key component of this agility.

Approaches to Innovation
There are many different approaches to innovation, but two of the most popular and effective are design thinking and lean startup.

Design Thinking
Design thinking is a human-centered approach to innovation that involves

understanding the needs and desires of customers and designing solutions to meet them. It involves a collaborative and iterative process that emphasizes empathy, experimentation, and creative problem-solving.

Design thinking involves several key stages, including empathy, define, ideate, prototype, and test. In the empathy stage, the focus is on understanding the needs and pain points of customers. In the define stage, the problem is clearly defined and a clear design challenge is established. In the ideate stage, brainstorming is used to generate a wide range of possible solutions. In the prototype stage, the best ideas are turned into tangible prototypes that can be tested with customers. Finally, in the test stage, the prototypes are evaluated to determine their effectiveness and potential for success.

Lean Startup

Lean startup is an approach to innovation that emphasizes rapid experimentation and iterative product development. It is based on the idea of creating a minimum viable product (MVP) that can be tested with customers to gather feedback and improve the product over time.

The lean startup process involves several key stages, including hypothesis, build, measure, and learn. In the hypothesis stage, a clear problem is identified, and a hypothesis is developed to solve it. In the build stage, an MVP is created that tests the hypothesis. In the measure stage, data is gathered on how customers use the MVP and how it can be improved. Finally, in the learn stage, the data is analyzed, and changes are made to the MVP based on customer feedback.

Both design thinking and lean startup are effective approaches to innovation that emphasize experimentation, collaboration, and rapid iteration. Companies that adopt these approaches are better able to create products and services that meet the needs of their customers and adapt to changing market conditions.

Conclusion
Innovation is critical to the success of any company in today's rapidly changing business environment. Companies that prioritize innovation are better able to adapt to shifting customer needs, anticipate new market trends, and stay ahead of their competitors. Two of the most popular and effective approaches to innovation are design thinking and lean startup, both of which emphasize experimentation, collaboration, and rapid iteration. By embracing these approaches, companies can create a culture of innovation that drives long-term success.

Chapter 12

Building a Company Culture

A company's culture is the collection of values, beliefs, attitudes, and behaviors that shape how people within the organization interact with one another and the outside world. It plays a crucial role in attracting and retaining top talent, fostering innovation, enhancing productivity, and ultimately, determining the success of the business. In this chapter, we'll explore the importance of building a positive company culture and how to create one that aligns with your business goals and values.

Why Building a Strong Company Culture is Crucial

A positive company culture can be a powerful differentiator in today's highly competitive business environment. Here are some of the key benefits of building a strong company culture:

Attract and retain top talent: A strong company culture can attract talented individuals who share your values and vision. It can also help retain your employees by creating a sense of belonging and purpose.

Foster innovation and creativity: A culture that values and rewards creativity, collaboration, and risk-taking can inspire employees to think outside the box and come up with innovative ideas.

Enhance productivity and engagement: Employees who feel valued, respected, and supported are more likely to be motivated, engaged, and productive. A positive culture can also create a sense of ownership and accountability.

Improve customer satisfaction: A company culture that prioritizes customer satisfaction and service can lead to better customer experiences, increased loyalty, and higher revenue.

Mitigate risk and promote ethical behavior: A strong culture can help prevent unethical behavior, such as fraud or harassment, by setting clear expectations and standards for behavior.

How to Build a Positive Company Culture

Building a positive company culture is a continuous process that requires commitment, effort, and leadership. Here are some steps you can take to create a culture that aligns with your business goals and values:

Define your values and mission: Your company's values and mission should reflect what you stand for and what you hope to achieve. They should guide all decisions and actions within the organization.

Communicate and reinforce your values: It's not enough to simply define your values and mission; you need to communicate them clearly and regularly to your employees. This can be done through company meetings, newsletters, training programs, and other channels.

Lead by example: Leaders set the tone for the entire organization. They should model the behaviors and attitudes they want to see in their employees.

Hire for cultural fit: When hiring new employees, it's important to look beyond their qualifications and experience. You should also consider whether they align with your company's values and mission.

Encourage collaboration and teamwork: A culture that values collaboration and teamwork can lead to better problem-solving, decision-making, and innovation. You can encourage this by creating cross-functional teams, organizing team-building activities, and recognizing and rewarding collaborative efforts.

Empower your employees: Empowering your employees means giving them the autonomy, resources, and support they need to do their best work. This can include offering training and development opportunities, providing feedback and recognition, and delegating responsibilities.

Celebrate successes and learn from failures: Celebrating successes and learning from failures can help create a culture of continuous improvement and resilience. You can do this by recognizing and rewarding achievements, sharing success stories, and conducting post-mortems after failures.

Conclusion

Building a positive company culture takes time and effort, but the benefits are well worth it. A strong culture can attract top talent, foster innovation, enhance productivity, and ultimately, drive the success of the business. By defining your values and mission, communicating them clearly, leading by example, hiring for cultural fit, encouraging collaboration and teamwork, empowering your employees, and celebrating successes and learning from failures, you can create a culture that aligns with your business goals and values.

Chapter 13

Case Studies

One of the most effective ways to learn about building a successful company is to study successful businesses that have already achieved it. In this chapter, we will explore several case studies of companies that have implemented different business models and strategies, examining what they did right and what you can learn from their successes.

Case Study 1: Amazon

Amazon is one of the most successful companies in the world, and its business model has been studied and emulated by many others. Amazon's key strategies include customer obsession, a vast selection of products, and a seamless customer experience.

One of the key factors in Amazon's success is its focus on the customer. Amazon has built its business around the idea that the customer comes first. It is constantly looking for ways to improve the customer experience, from offering fast and free shipping to providing personalized product recommendations.

Another important element of Amazon's success is its vast selection of products. Amazon offers everything from books and electronics to groceries and clothing, and it is constantly adding new products to its inventory. This has helped Amazon become the go-to destination for online shopping for millions of people around the world.

Finally, Amazon has invested heavily in building a seamless customer experience. The company's website is easy to use, and it offers features like one-click ordering and easy returns to make the buying process as easy as possible for customers.

Case Study 2: Airbnb

Airbnb is a platform that allows people to rent out their homes or apartments to travelers. Its business model is built around the idea of sharing, and it has become hugely successful in a relatively short amount of time.

One of the key factors in Airbnb's success is its focus on the user experience. The company's website and mobile app are easy to use, and the company offers a range of services to help hosts and guests make the most of their experience.

Another important element of Airbnb's success is its community of hosts and guests. The company has built a strong community of users who are passionate about the idea of sharing their homes and exploring new places.

Finally, Airbnb has been successful in attracting a diverse range of hosts and guests. The company has worked hard to make sure that people from all walks of life feel welcome on the platform, and it has taken steps to ensure that hosts and guests feel safe and secure when using the platform.

Case Study 3: Tesla

Tesla is a company that is revolutionizing the automotive industry with its electric cars. Its business model is built around the idea of sustainable transportation, and it has become a leader in the industry in a relatively short amount of time.

One of the key factors in Tesla's success is its focus on innovation. The company has invested heavily in research and development, and it has been successful in creating electric cars that are not only environmentally friendly, but also stylish and fun to drive.

Another important element of Tesla's success is its focus on building a strong brand. Tesla has positioned itself as a company that is at the forefront of innovation, and it has built a loyal following of customers who are passionate about the company's products and mission.

Finally, Tesla has been successful in building a strong network of partners and suppliers. The company has worked with a range of suppliers to develop its electric car technology, and it has also built a network of charging stations to support its customers.

Conclusion:

In this chapter, we have explored three case studies of successful businesses that have implemented different business models and strategies. While each of these companies is unique, they all share some common elements, including a focus on the customer experience, a commitment to innovation, and a strong brand. By studying these successful companies, you can gain valuable insights into what it takes to build a successful business and apply these lessons to your own company.

Chapter 14

Future Trends

The world of business is constantly evolving, and it's important for companies to stay ahead of the curve in order to remain competitive. In this final chapter, we will explore some of the key future trends in business models and strategies, and provide insights on how companies can adapt and thrive in the years to come.

Emphasis on Sustainability and Social Responsibility: As the world becomes increasingly aware of the impact of climate change and social issues, businesses are expected to take on a more active role in addressing these concerns. Companies that prioritize sustainability and social responsibility are likely to have a competitive advantage in the future, as consumers and investors alike become more conscious of the environmental and social impact of their choices.

Shift towards Subscription-based Models: With the rise of subscription-based services such as Netflix, Amazon Prime, and Spotify, many businesses are beginning to adopt this model as a way to generate recurring revenue. Subscription-based models offer benefits such as predictable revenue, reduced customer acquisition costs, and increased customer loyalty. This trend is expected to continue in the future, with more companies across different industries adopting subscription-based models.

Increasing Importance of Data Analytics: As data becomes increasingly accessible, businesses are starting to realize the value of data analytics in driving decision-making and improving operational efficiency. The use of artificial intelligence and machine learning is also becoming more widespread, as companies seek to gain insights into consumer behavior, improve product development, and streamline supply chain management.

Rise of the Sharing Economy: The sharing economy, which allows individuals to share resources such as cars, homes, and equipment, has disrupted traditional industries such as hospitality and transportation. This trend is expected to continue, with more companies exploring the potential of the sharing economy as a business model.

Growth of E-commerce: With the increasing popularity of online shopping, e-commerce is becoming an increasingly important sales channel for businesses. This trend is expected to continue, with the rise of mobile commerce and the growing popularity of social commerce.

Importance of Personalization: As consumers become more demanding, businesses are starting to focus on personalization as a way to stand out from the competition. The use of data analytics and artificial intelligence is making it easier for companies to deliver personalized experiences to customers, such as customized product recommendations and targeted marketing campaigns.

Increasing Emphasis on Employee Well-being: As companies compete for top talent, there is a growing recognition of the importance of employee well-being. Businesses are starting to invest in employee wellness programs, flexible working arrangements, and other initiatives to improve the work-life balance of their employees.

Adoption of New Technologies: The rapid pace of technological change means that businesses need to be agile and adaptable in order to stay ahead of the curve. Technologies such as blockchain, 5G, and virtual reality are expected to have a significant impact on businesses in the future, and companies that are quick to adopt and leverage these technologies are likely to have a competitive advantage.

In order to stay ahead of the curve and succeed in the future, businesses will need to be flexible, adaptable, and willing to experiment with new ideas and strategies. The future of business is likely to be shaped by a combination of technological innovation, changing consumer behavior, and a growing focus on sustainability and social responsibility. Companies that are able to navigate these trends and capitalize on emerging opportunities are likely to be the most successful in the years to come.